An Invitation to

Centering Prayer

wed. 04/27/05

as a "love word" or mantra
use :

"Remain in me, as I remain in you"

— John 15:4

"As the father loves me, so I also
love you. Remain in my love."

— John 15:9

use
love word " Remain in me."
for
meditating

Wed. 04/27/05 c. 12:00 noon
   "As The Father loves me, so I also love you.
    Remain in my love."   (John 15:9-10)
Oh, if I only could feel Jesus' love - perhaps
Centering prayer and meditation will help me feel His love,
I who hate myself so.

"What we have to learn when we meditate
 is <u>some glimmer of an insight into our
 own value and importance</u>.   (emphasis mine)

"We learn in meditation That The source of
 faith is The Spirit of Jesus dwelling in
 our heart.

".. Meditating is simply uncovering
  the love that is God in our own hearts."

           Fr. John Main, O.S.B.
           <u>The Way of Unknowing</u>
excerpted from "Living Faith" Wednesday, April 27, 2005

An
Invitation
to

Centering Prayer

M. Basil Pennington, O.C.S.O.

Including an
Introduction to *Lectio Divina*

Luke Dysinger, O.S.B.

Liguori
LIGUORI, MISSOURI

Imprimi Potest
Richard Thibodeau, C.Ss.R.
Provincial, Denver Province
The Redemptorists

Published by Liguori Publications
Liguori, Missouri
www.liguori.org

Library of Congress Cataloging-in-Publication Data

Pennington, M. Basil.
    An invitation to centering prayer : including an introduction to lectio divina / M. Basil Pennington.
       p. cm.
    Rev. ed. of: The way back home. c1989.
    Includes bibliographical references.
    ISBN 0-7648-0782-X
    1. Contemplation. I. Pennington, M. Basil. Way back home. II. Title.

BV5091.C7 .P45 2001
248.3'4—dc21   2001038667

Printed in the United States of America
08 07 06 05 04   6 5 4 3 2
Revised edition 2001

Contents

Appendices

Preface

This volume is really the work of our good editor, John Cleary. It reflects an important evolution that has taken place in what is popularly called the "Centering Prayer Movement."

In 1971 Pope Paul VI asked us monks to do what we could to help the Church re-find its contemplative dimension for, as he said, there can never be a true renewal in depth without this. After a time of prayer and reflection we began to teach, in as simple a way as we could, an ancient Christian way of entering into contemplative prayer. As is our tradition, we always put contemplative prayer in its fuller context: a context of faith and love nourished constantly by the Word of God. But at that time most were keenly interested in finding a simple way to "meditate" and showed little interest in what is traditionally called *lectio* or *lectio divina*, meeting the Lord in the inspired Word and letting God speak to us and reveal Godself to us and draw us into a communion of faith and love.

The ancient way of entering into contemplative prayer, which has traditionally been called Prayer of the Heart, when presented in a very simple, modern way soon received the name Centering Prayer. In response to the desires of those years we produced a number of books, such as *Centering Prayer*, which presented the history of this way of prayer and gave practical instruction on how to enter into it. Centering Prayer became very popular. Not only were the books translated into many languages but there was a constant demand for new books. In response we produced *Centered Living*, *Call to the Center*, and others. Finally a member of the Ecumenical Institute of Spirituality challenged me to write a very simple book that would be suitable for high-school students. In response to this challenge I produced a very short, simple book: *The Way Back Home*. Hardly larger than a pamphlet and actually printed as a pamphlet by the

Union Church, many thousands of copies were distributed over the years.

But not unsurprisingly to us, after practicing Centering Prayer for some time, many began to show an increasing interest in its fuller context and especially in *lectio divina*, which nourishes the roots of contemplative prayer. In response to this interest and desire we produced books such as *Lectio Divina: Renewing the Ancient Practice of Praying the Scriptures* and *Awake in the Spirit*. Now John Cleary, as an editor in touch with the interests and needs of the Christian community, has taken in hand our little book, *The Way Back Home*, and has added to it a simple presentation of *lectio divina*, drawn in good part from my book on lectio. However, as I acknowledged in that book, much of this particular material was drawn from or inspired by the writings of Father Luke Dysinger, O.S.B.

So I want to express here a very sincere word of thanks to both John Cleary and to Father Luke for the contribution they have made to this volume. It is my hope that this little book proves very useful to many, leading them into the joys of *lectio* and contemplation. A great Father of the Church said: "Our hearts are made for you,

O Lord, and they will not rest until they rest in you." How will our restless hearts find that place of rest they seek, except by finding God. Not finding out about God, but by finding God, experiencing God, coming to know God by experience. This is what true *lectio* leads us to, when we receive the Word and let it expand our consciousness and lead us into the spaces of divine contemplation. May this little book, short and simple though it be, prove to be for many a key that opens up this traditional Christian way to higher consciousness, a consciousness in accord with who we are as men and women baptized into Christ and made partakers of the divine nature and life, made to be true friends of God in Christ.

M. BASIL PENNINGTON, O.C.S.O.
HOLY SPIRIT ABBEY, CONYERS, GEORGIA
JULY 2001

Centering Prayer

Lord, Where Are You?

H istory repeats itself. We've all heard that. We ask the same questions others have asked before us. We seek the same things others have sought before us:

A meaning for our lives,
friends,
and some kind of relationship
with God that
grounds all the rest.

We look for a wise person who has some answers and who shows by the peace in his eyes and the serene joy in his face that these are answers that work.

In recent years a lot of men and women have headed to the Far East in search of those answers. They have gone off to India, Thailand, and even more exotic places. Some have found something, but most have returned home to their own roots.

This isn't the first time men and women have gone east. Remember Marco Polo, Mateo Ricci, and Francis Xavier? In the Middle Ages there were crusaders and pilgrims. Earlier there were other seekers. My patron Basil and his friend Gregory left the lecture halls of Athens in the fourth century to find a truer, deeper wisdom. John Cassian, the wealthy young man from Dalmatia, went the same way. Women, too: Paula and that delightful pair, Malenia the Elder and Malenia the Younger, a grandmother and granddaughter, sought this deeper wisdom.

We see this "seeking" back in Jesus' time. What were the two young fishermen from the shores of Lake Galilee doing east of the Jordan? They were seeking a strange man who had emerged from the desert. He had long hair and a long beard; he wore a camel's pelt, and it was said he ate only wild honey and chewed on grasshoppers! But he had a message. And people were flocking to him. John and Andrew went, too. "Are you the one?" they asked—the one who has the answers, the one we all hope for.

This man from the desert, John the Baptizer, was a humble man. "No, I am not he. But wait, prepare. He is coming."

John and Andrew did wait. Then suddenly one day, as the Baptizer was preaching, he lifted up his eyes and saw him. "Look! Look there! There he is." John and Andrew took off. As they ran up behind Jesus, the master turned. And he asked them what he asks each one of us—these are the first recorded words of Jesus to his disciples—"What do you want? What are you looking for?"

What is our answer?

John was a smart young man. He wanted it all. "Master, where do you dwell?" He didn't want any particular little thing. He wanted to move right in with the Lord.

Jesus replied, "Come and see."

And they followed Jesus.

Probably John and Andrew fully expected Jesus to lead them to some house or small hut where they could stay with him to learn all the secrets of true happiness and divine wisdom. But soon enough they learned that while the foxes have their dens and the birds their nests, the Son of Man had nowhere to lay his head.

John followed Jesus faithfully for three years. He listened to his every word. He came to know that he was the disciple Jesus loved—just as each of us will discover if we spend some time with Jesus.

Finally a momentous night came. At first John did not know its full import, but at Jesus' command he and Andrew's brother, Simon Peter, prepared a special meal. At that meal Jesus opened his heart to John and the others in a way he never had before. And as he did, he finally answered John's first question.

"He who loves me, the Father and I will come and we will dwell in him." Where do I dwell, John? I dwell in you.

This is God's favorite dwelling place on earth: in you and in me.

God is everywhere, of course, but where does God *dwell?* The word "dwell" which John and Jesus used has a special meaning. It doesn't just mean being there or living there, but being there with all the intimacy of loved ones or family. God dwells in us. God wants to share life intimately with us. That is the reason for the whole creation. "All things are yours, and you are Christ's and Christ is God's."

God dwells with us. God is always at home within us. But, alas, most of the time *we are not home*.

The True Self

When we were born—of course, most of us don't remember it for ourselves, though it is all written deep in our memories—we experienced ourselves as little bundles of need. We needed warmth, we needed stroking, we needed nurture. All these *things* were very important to us. And we yowled to get them.

And most of us got them.

Our consciousness expanded. The *persons* who supplied these needs became very important to us. There was a deep bonding.

As we grew and our consciousness continued to expand, we became aware of how important were the things we did, our *doings*.

We learned that if we acted in a certain way, people would give us what we wanted. If we kept certain people happy with the way we acted, rewards would be forthcoming. And we would be the envy of others.

Gradually out of all of this came a sense of self—unfortunately a false sense of self. We saw ourselves as what we had, what we could do, what others thought of us.

That's how most of us still see ourselves, most of the time.

Have you ever noticed how often, when a man introduces himself, he immediately tells you what he does. And when he doesn't, how quickly do you ask him that question: What do you do? That's why it is so difficult for many men to retire—they have so identified themselves with what they do that to no longer do it is like losing a big part of themselves.

In the past, women didn't do this so much. They weren't thought to do anything significant, being just housewives and mothers. (What a strange sense of values we sometimes have!) They often identified with what they had: their clothes, their jewelry, their hair. But it was the same false sense of self showing up.

Times have changed, of course. Today, Mrs. Jones is apt to be president of the company while Mr. Jones may be wearing his gold bracelet, neck chain, and even earrings.

It is a very fragile image, made up of what we have, what we do, and what other people think of us. We can so easily lose things, lose our ability to perform, lose our hold on others. We tend to be very defensive.

We tend to be competitive. After all, the more he gets, the less I get. The more they like her, the less they are going to like me and take care of me.

This false sense of self leads to frustration and even to violence. If I sense that I must always do what others want, that I must please them to get what I want, deep down I resent it. I even hate them. Of course, I can't admit that, even to myself. I have to keep pleasing them to keep getting what I want and need.

So I repress my resentment and live with frustration. And then one day we come to our senses....

Our false sense of self flows over into our experience of God. For many people God is just the big one out there somewhere, the giver of the real goodies that last forever. We have to satisfy him, or else. This is their sense of religion: satisfying God to get what they want—and resenting God for making such demands on them.

But all of this is not the reality. It is not who we really are. It is not the way things really are.

God is not somebody out there who is going to give us eternal goodies. God is a loving friend who dwells within us, wanting us to dwell within so that God can teach us all things and, above all, tell us of God's love.

We want to come to see our true selves, that self who dwells in God's creative love. At our center we are not empty, needy little things. At our center we are full, very full— full of God with all his creative love.

We don't have to care about what other people think of us. God thinks the world of us—he made the world just for us. "All things are yours, and you are Christ's, and Christ is God's." We can do whatever we want: "I can do all things in him who strengthens me." We can have whatever we want: "Ask and you shall receive."

We want to truly experience our selves. We want to discover not only how rich and powerful and beautiful we are—discover how much we are loved, because God does dwell with us as a most loving friend and teacher and Lord.

But how do we come home?

Coming Home

One of the young men who headed east in the course of the fifth century was a wealthy young man from Dalmatia who had gone to Rome to study—John Cassian by name. John traveled widely in what we call today Asia Minor and Syria, and finally he settled in a monastery near Bethlehem. But he was far from satisfied. He set out again on a seven-year quest only to return to his monastery still filled with longing. His third journey took him into the depths of the Egyptian desert where he sought out the fabled fathers of the desert. There he came upon a wise old man who was said to be the holiest, oldest, and wisest of the fathers: Abba Isaac.

John and his traveling companion Little Herman approached the venerable father with their deepest need. "Father, give us a word on prayer." The venerable abba spoke to them beautifully of communion with the God who so loves us and dwells within us. He spoke of the fruits and the joy to be found in a life that is grounded on the inner experience of God.

John and his friend all but floated back to the guest cell that night. But when they awoke in the morning their feet were again well planted on the earth. Little Herman turned to John: "Yes, but how do you do it?" How does one enter into the experience of the living God who lives within us and grounds our lives upon the reality of who we really are deep down?

The two young men picked up their tunics and ran back across the sands to the cell of Abba Isaac. "How do you do it? How do you enter into this kind of prayer?"

The father was impressed by the sincerity of his two inquirers. "I see that you are true

seekers. Then let me tell you what I learned
as a young man from one of the holiest, oldest, and wisest fathers." Thus began Abba
Isaac's second conference and the practical
teaching on how to enter into the space of
the heart and come into the presence of the
living God who lives within.

John did not return to his Bethlehem
monastery. He went instead to the capital of
his world, Constantinople. There he was or-
dained a priest and set forth to bring to the
West the wisdom he had found in the East.
John founded two monasteries near the city
of Marseilles, one for men and one for women.
For these monks and nuns he wrote down as
best he could remember the words of life he
had received from the great spiritual masters
of the East. It is here we find the second conference of Abba Isaac with its practical instruction on Christian meditation, the method we
call today "Centering Prayer."

Through the ages monks and nuns read
the conferences of Abba Isaac as recorded by
John Cassian. They practiced the prayer. And

they taught others the prayer. Spiritual fathers in the monasteries and lay brothers out on the granges and at the fairs taught the prayer. The fathers wrote treatises on it for their spiritual sons and daughters. The best known of these, by far, is one written in the fourteenth century, *The Cloud of Unknowing.* It is still widely used in our times, available in several editions.

In 1971 there was an important gathering of spiritual fathers in Rome. These were the Cistercian abbots, the leaders of monasteries from all parts of the world. They had come to reflect together on how they could better serve their sons and daughters. They gathered around the Holy Father, Pope Paul VI. The aging pontiff had one message for them. While remaining faithful to their own monastic way, he urged them to do all they could to help all the sons and daughters of the Church, all the pilgrim people of God, to rediscover this ancient way of prayer, to discover their hearts centered in God so that they could ground their lives in truth—the really real—and in love and in the power of God. That is where fullness and fulfillment lie for us all.

The Cistercians sought a simple practical way of sharing this prayer. Soon they were teaching it widely. Inspired by one of the greatest spiritual masters among them, Father Louis (Thomas Merton) the prayer began to be called Centering Prayer—a new name for a very old reality.

Here then, in its modern form, is the ancient method of Christian meditation that Abba Isaac taught John Cassian and which the Cistercian (Trappist) spiritual fathers teach today:

Centering Prayer

Sit relaxed and quiet.

1. Be in faith and love to God, who dwells in the center of your being.
2. Take up a love word and let it be gently present, supporting your being to God in faith-filled love.

3. Whenever you become aware of anything else, simply, gently return to the Lord with the use of your prayer word.

At the end of your prayer time let the Our Father (or some other prayer) pray itself within you.

SIT RELAXED AND QUIET

Our friends have brought back some wonderful postures from the East such as the lotus and half lotus. They are good ways to sit for meditation. But for most of us simply sitting in a chair, one that gives our back good support, is probably best. The important thing is that we are relaxed (but not too relaxed or we will soon be snoring) and that our back is straight so that the vitalizing energies can flow easily. It is good to close our eyes. We use a good bit of psychic energy in seeing. As soon as we close our eyes we begin to quiet down.

Jesus has said to us: "Come to me, all you who labor and are heavily burdened, and I will refresh you." Prayer should be refreshing—physically as well as spiritually and psychically.

Be in faith and love to God who dwells in the center of your being.

We know that the Lord dwells in us. We know that by faith: because Jesus said it, it is so.

In love we give ourselves to God, our whole attention, all that we are, for the twenty minutes of our prayer. "I am all yours, Lord. Do with me whatever you will."

Take up a love word and let it be gently present, supporting your being to God in faith-filled love.

We choose a word of love, usually our favorite name for the Lord: "Jesus," "Lord," "Friend." (Probably Jesus' love word was "Abba.") We gently say this word deep within, and let it quietly repeat itself. No effort. Just let it be there—to keep us there with the

Lord—open to the Lord, letting God be present to us in any way God wants.

Whenever you become aware of anything else, simply, gently return to the Lord with the use of your prayer word.

We settle down with the Lord. It is very peaceful. Then all of sudden we realize we are thinking about what we had for supper last night, or something we forgot to do, or our plans for next summer, or, or, or…. The interior computer keeps going. Also there are the things from outside: we hear voices from the next room, somebody is mowing a lawn or playing the piano down the hall, and so on.

Each time we become *aware* of something, we use our love word to return gently to the Lord. Some days we will have to use that word almost constantly. There is a lot going on inside—or outside. Other days we will not need it much at all. It doesn't really matter, just as long as each time we become *aware* of anything, we gently return to the Lord.

As we do, we let the other thing go. It is as if the Lord were asking us: "Do you love me more than this?" With our love word we say: "Yes." For these twenty minutes we let everything else go and just give God the space of our lives, so that God can do what God wills. And what God wills most of all is to let us know how much we are loved, how truly God is with us—all the way.

As we choose the Lord and these things float away, all the stress and strain around them float away, too. After the prayer we will be able to attend to them without all that "stuff" around them. This is how our Lord refreshes us psychologically during this prayer, even while we are refreshed physically and spiritually.

So let them go, let them flow—anything and everything that comes up for us—while we just gently and simply use our word of love and choose the Lord.

At the end of your prayer time let the Our Father (or some other prayer) pray itself within you.

There are many people who pray this way regularly, centering twice a day. They have found that *twenty minutes* is a good time to spend in this prayer. It is enough to sort of let go of all the stress and tension that have accumulated since the last meditation and to get a good refreshing rest in the Lord—and to give the Lord time to do some deeper healing if he wants. So we strongly recommend twenty minutes.

Twice a day. We don't meditate just to enjoy twenty minutes of bliss. We want that shift of consciousness wherein we become more fully aware of our self and God and live out of that reality. We want to live centered lives that freely hold everybody and everything in love—lives that are empowered by the Lord at the center of our being. This shift comes about much more quickly if we do spend time at the center twice a day rather than just once a day.

So: *twenty minutes, twice a day*.

Let us come home to dwell with the Lord.

It Begins With Faith

T through this little book we have been listening to the Lord. Jesus has told us that
he and the Father dwell with us, that they
want to refresh us, that all things are ours and
we are God's. We can believe all that, we know
it is all true, because God has given us the gift
we call faith.

Faith is the ability the Lord gives us to
know something is true because God has said
it. It is a precious gift because it lets us in on a
whole lot—really, on the whole story: "I have
made known to you all that my Father has
made known to me."

Like our muscles or our minds, faith is a
gift that grows by use. Faith comes from hear-

ing and it grows by hearing. Each day we want to grow in faith. "The just person (and the happy one) lives by faith." Each day we want to hear the Word of God and receive it.

Here is a very simple traditional way of doing this:

Sacred Reading

It is well to keep the sacred Scriptures enthroned in our home in a place of honor as a real presence of the Word in our midst.

1. Take the sacred text with reverence and call upon the Holy Spirit.
2. For five minutes (or longer, if you are so drawn) listen to the Lord speaking to you through the text, and respond.
3. At the end of the time, choose a word or phrase (perhaps one will have been "given" to you) different from your Centering Prayer word to take with you, and thank the Lord for being with you and speaking to you.

The place we can most easily hear the Lord is in the Scriptures.

The Bible should be among our most precious possessions. It should never be simply left lying about or shelved among the other books. Rather it should be enthroned in our homes and offices as a real presence of the Lord in our midst.

Each day we want to take some time to listen to the Lord speaking to us in this inspired word.

We take up our Bible with great reverence, aware of God's presence. We kiss the Bible and ask the Holy Spirit who inspired the writer and who lives in us to make the word come alive now in us.

Then we listen for our allotted time. If the Lord speaks to us in the first word, we respond. If not, we just move gently on, listening, ready to respond. If the Lord speaks powerfully to us, we simply abide in this word and presence.

At the end of our time, we thank the Lord (isn't it wonderful we can have God speak to us whenever we want!) and we take away from our encounter a thought or word to carry with us through the day.

Some days the Lord speaks a word to us, gives it to us. We don't have to take one. God's word comes alive and in its liveliness enlivens us.

Other days, the Lord seems absent. We read one word after the other and nothing speaks to us. It is then, at the end of our reading/listening, that we choose a word to carry with us. Oftentimes I have found that this proves to be just the word someone else needs from me as the day moves on. Other times I find that the chosen word suddenly comes alive—a real encounter with the risen Lord— when I least expect it.

At the Last Supper, Jesus told his disciples (and told all of us): I no longer call you servants, but *friends,* because I make known to you all that the Father has made known to me—all the secrets of my heart.

We have been made for a deep intimate friendship with the Lord. Our hearts long for it. As a great sinner who became a great saint once cried: "Our hearts are made for you, O Lord, and they will not rest until they rest in you!"

We are not content with just listening to the Lord's words, no matter how wonderful they are. We want a deeper, more experiential union with God. It is like any true friendship: as it grows it needs to go beyond words to doing things together and for each other. The image God has frequently used is that of the marital embrace, that total being to each other. We need those times of Centering Prayer when we listen not just with our ears, our eyes, our minds but more with our hearts, with our whole being.

Faith is the gateway to intimacy. And faith grows by hearing.

The Prodigal Father

As Jesus spoke a very mixed crowd gathered around. On the fringes were the big shots, the Pharisees who had all the answers, the scribes who knew the law, and the priests, the holy ones. They looked down on the motley crew pressing in to hear Jesus—a sinful crowd that did not know the law.

What was more painful to Jesus was the fact that many of the poor little ones who were listening to him readily believed that they were indeed the sinful ones. They knew their sins too well. They longed to hear words that would bring them peace.

Jesus told them then this story.

A rich man had two sons. The older was a

very righteous lad, painfully faithful to his duties. He knew he was the firstborn son and heir and took good care of his future inheritance. The younger had other interests in life. He wanted to live to the full.

He asked his good father for whatever money might be coming to him so that he could get on with life. Poor, foolish lad. He chased the pleasures of the moment. A false self-image had him in its grips. He let others play up to him and live off him. Eventually they went away and left him an unhappy pauper. Ill prepared for life, he could only get the most menial and humiliating jobs.

Finally he came to himself. Deep down he knew his true dignity, his true worth, as the son of his good father. He had forfeited every claim to that dignity. But at least he could throw himself on that good father's mercy—and get a better shake than he was getting out on his own.

So home he headed.

The good father's love had never faltered. Nor had the keen eye of love dimmed. From afar he spied his son, and despite all his age and dignity he ran out to meet the poor little tramp to welcome him home with great love and joy. He had no time for the poor lad's sad tale, at least not now in this moment of newfound joy. There was time only for love and joy and celebration. The past was to be fully forgotten. His son was home—that is all he wanted.

Deep down, I guess all of us question our worthiness. No matter what has been our track record—whether we have some terrible mistakes on our record or just the miserable little collection of human mess-ups that is the common lot of every child of God—we question whether it could really be true: that God loves me, dwells in me, really wants to be my friend, really wants me to be an intimate friend.

That's why Jesus told this story. We are all, in one way or another, prodigals. But God is even more prodigal in a generous forgiving love for us. We have gone off, one way or another. But God has stayed at home—in us— waiting for us to return.

It is time to return home.

The way is simple.

Very simple. We like to do things that are really hard. Then we can pat ourselves on the back for having accomplished them. (But that's just the false self-image bragging again.)

But Jesus has said: "Unless you become as a little one, you can not enter the kingdom."

The kingdom of God is within.

Come in. Come home. The kingdom is our home. We are the children of the king.

Within we find love. Within we find peace.

Within we find our true self, that beautiful person whom God loves so much.

Come home to yourself. Come home to your God.

Lectio Divina

The Process
of Lectio Divina

A very ancient art, practiced at one time by all Christians, is the technique known as *lectio divina*—a slow, contemplative praying of the Scriptures which enables the Bible, the Word of God, to become a means of union with God. This ancient practice has been kept alive in the Christian monastic tradition, enabling us to discover in our daily life an underlying spiritual rhythm. Within this rhythm we discover an increasing ability to offer more of ourselves to God, and to accept the embrace that God is continuously extending to us in the person of the Son Jesus Christ.

Lectio
(reading/listening)

The art of *lectio divina* begins with cultivating the ability to listen deeply, to hear "with the ear of our hearts" as Saint Benedict encourages us in the Prologue to the Rule. When we read the Scriptures we should try to imitate the prophet Elijah. We should allow ourselves to become women and men who are able to listen for the still, small voice of God (1 Kings 19:12); the "faint murmuring sound" which is God's word for us, God's voice touching our hearts. This gentle listening is an "atunement" to the presence of God in that special part of God's creation which is the Scriptures.

The cry of the prophets to ancient Israel was the joy-filled command to "Listen!" "Sh'ma Israel: Hear, O Israel!" In *lectio divina* we, too, heed that command and turn to the Scriptures, knowing that we must "hear"—listen—to the voice of God, which often speaks very softly. In order to hear someone speaking softly we must learn to be silent. We must learn to love silence. If we are constantly speaking or if we are surrounded with noise, we cannot hear gentle sounds. The practice of *lectio divina*, therefore, requires that we first quiet down in order to hear God's word to us. This is the first step of *lectio divina*, appropriately called *lectio*—reading.

The reading or listening which is the first step in *lectio divina* is very different from the speed reading which modern Christians apply to newspapers, books, and even to the Bible. *Lectio* is reverential listening; listening both in a spirit of silence and of awe. We are listening for the still, small voice of God that will speak to us personally—not loudly, but intimately. In *lectio* we read slowly, attentively, gently listening to hear a word or phrase that is God's word for us this day.

Meditatio
(meditation)

Once we have found a word or a passage in the Scriptures which speaks to us in a personal way, we must take it in and "ruminate" on it. The image of the ruminant animal quietly chewing its cud was used in antiquity as a symbol of the Christian pondering the Word of God. Christians have always seen a scriptural invitation to *lectio divina* in the example of the Virgin Mary "pondering in her heart" what she saw and heard of Christ (see Lk 2:19). For us today these images are a reminder that we must take in the word—that is, memorize it—and while gently repeating it to ourselves, allow it to interact with our thoughts, our hopes, our memories, our desires. This is the second step or stage in *lectio divina—meditatio*. Through *meditatio* we allow God's word to become God's word for us, a word that touches us and affects us at our deepest levels.

Oratio
(prayer)

The third step in *lectio divina* is *oratio*—prayer: prayer understood both as dialogue with God, that is, as loving conversation with the One who has invited us into an embrace; and as consecration, prayer as the priestly offering to God of parts of ourselves that we have not previously believed God wants. In this consecration-prayer we allow the word that we have taken in and on which we are pondering to touch and change our deepest selves. Just as a priest consecrates the elements of bread and wine at the Eucharist, God invites us in *lectio divina* to hold up our most difficult and pain-filled experiences to God, and to gently recite over them the healing word or phrase God has given us in our *lectio* and *meditatio*. In this *oratio*, this consecration-prayer, we allow our real selves to be touched and changed by the word of God.

Contemplatio
(contemplation)

Finally, we simply rest in the presence of the One who has used the word as a means of inviting us to accept a transforming embrace. No one who has ever been in love needs to be reminded that there are moments in loving relationships when words are unnecessary. It is the same in our relationship with God. Wordless, quiet rest in the presence of the One Who loves us has a name in the Christian tradition—*contemplatio*, contemplation. Once again we practice silence, letting go of our own words; this time simply enjoying the experience of being in the presence of God.

The Underlying Rhythm of Lectio Divina

If we are to practice *lectio divina* effectively, we must travel back in time to an understanding that today is in danger of being almost completely lost. In the Christian past the words *action* (or *practice*, from the Greek *praktikos*) and *contemplation* did not describe different kinds of Christians engaging (or not engaging) in different forms of prayer and apostolates. Practice and contemplation were understood as the two poles of our underlying, ongoing spiritual rhythm: a gentle oscillation back and forth between spiritual "activity" with regard to God and "receptivity."

Practice—spiritual "activity"—referred in ancient times to our active cooperation with God's grace in rooting out vices and allowing the virtues to flourish. The direction of spiritual activity was not outward in the sense of an apostolate, but *inward*—down into the depths of the soul where the Spirit of God is constantly transforming us, refashioning us in God's image. The *active life* is thus coming to see who we truly are and allowing ourselves to be remade into what God intends us to become.

In the early monastic tradition *contemplation* was understood in two ways. First was *theoria physike,* the contemplation of God in creation—God in "the many." Second was *theologia,* the contemplation of God in Godself without images or words—God as "The One." From this perspective *lectio divina* serves as a training-ground for the contemplation of God in creation.

In contemplation we cease from interior spiritual *doing* and learn simply to *be*, that is to rest in the presence of our loving Father.

Just as we constantly move back and forth in our exterior lives between speaking and listening, between questioning and reflecting, so in our spiritual lives we must learn to enjoy the refreshment of simply *being* in God's presence, an experience that naturally alternates (if we let it!) with our spiritual *practice*.

In ancient times contemplation was not regarded as a goal to be achieved through some method of prayer, but was simply accepted with gratitude as God's recurring gift. At intervals the Lord invites us to cease from speaking so that we can simply rest in his embrace. This is the pole of our inner spiritual rhythm called contemplation.

How different this ancient understanding is from our modern approach! Instead of recognizing that we all gently oscillate back and forth between spiritual activity and receptivity, between practice and contemplation, we today tend to set contemplation before ourselves as a goal—something we imagine we can achieve through some spiritual technique. We must be willing to sacrifice our "goal-oriented" approach if we are to practice *lectio divina*, because *lectio divina* has no other goal than spending time with God through the medium of the Word. The amount of time we spend in any aspect of *lectio divina*, whether it be rumination, consecration, or contemplation depends on God's Spirit, not on us. *Lectio divina* teaches us to savor and delight in all the different flavors of God's presence, whether they be active or receptive modes of experiencing God.

In *lectio divina* we offer ourselves to God; and we are people in motion. In ancient times this inner spiritual motion was described as a helix—an ascending spiral. Viewed in only two dimensions it appears as a circular motion back and forth; seen with the added dimension of time it becomes a helix, an ascending spiral by means of which we are drawn ever closer to God. The whole of our spiritual lives were viewed in this way, as a gentle oscillation between spiritual activity and receptivity by means of which God unites us ever closer. In just the same way the steps or stages of *lectio divina* represent an oscillation back and forth between these spiritual poles. In *lectio divina* we recognize our underlying spiritual rhythm and discover many different ways of experiencing God's presence—many different ways of praying.

The Practice of Lectio Divina

Private *Lectio Divina*

Choose a text of the Scriptures that you wish to pray. Many Christians use in their daily *lectio divina* one of the readings from the eucharistic liturgy for the day; others prefer to slowly work through a particular book of the Bible. It makes no difference which text is chosen, as long as one has no set goal of "covering" a certain amount of text: the amount of text "covered" is in God's hands, not yours.

Place yourself in a comfortable position

and allow yourself to become silent. Some Christians focus for a few moments on their breathing; other have a beloved "prayer word" or "prayer phrase" they gently recite in order to become interiorly silent. For some Centering Prayer makes a good, brief introduction to *lectio divina*. Use whatever method is best for you and allow yourself to enjoy silence for a few moments.

Then turn to the text and read it slowly, gently. Savor each portion of the reading, constantly listening for the "still, small voice" of a word or phrase that somehow says, "I am for you today." Do not expect lightening or ecstasies. In *lectio divina* God is teaching us to listen to God, to seek God in silence. God does not reach out and grab us; rather, God softly, gently invites us ever more deeply into God's presence.

Next take the word or phrase into yourself. Memorize it and slowly repeat it to yourself, allowing it to interact with your inner world of concerns, memories, and ideas. Do not be afraid of "distractions." Memories or thoughts are simply parts of yourself which, when they rise up during *lectio divina*, are asking to be given to God along with the rest of your inner self. Allow this inner pondering, this rumination, to invite you into dialogue with God.

Then, speak to God. Whether you use words or ideas or images or all three is not important. Interact with God as you would with one who you know loves and accepts you. And give to God what you have discovered in yourself during your experience of *meditatio*. Experience yourself as the priest that you are. Experience God using the word or phrase that God has given you as a means of blessing, of transforming the ideas and memories, which your pondering on the Word has awakened. Give to God what you have found within your heart.

Finally, simply rest in God's embrace. And when God invites you to return to your pondering of the Word or to your inner dialogue with God, do so. Learn to use words when words are helpful, and to let go of words when they are no longer necessary. Rejoice in the knowledge that God is with you both in words and silence, in spiritual activity and inner receptivity.

Sometimes in *lectio divina* one will return several times to the printed text, either to savor the literary context of the word or phrase that God has given, or to seek a new word or phrase to ponder. At other times only a single word or phrase will fill the whole time set aside for *lectio divina*. It is not necessary to anxiously assess the quality of one's *lectio divina* as if one were "performing" or seeking some goal: *lectio divina* has no goal other than that of being in the presence of God by praying the Scriptures.

Lectio Divina as a Group Exercise

In the churches of the Third World where books are rare, a form of corporate *lectio divina* is becoming common in which a text from the Scriptures is pondered by Christians praying together in a group. This form of *lectio divina* works best in a group of between four and eight people. A group leader coordinates the process and facilitates sharing. The same text from the Scriptures is read out three times, followed each time by a period of silence and an opportunity for each member of the group to share the fruit of his or her *lectio*.

The first reading (the text is actually read twice on this occasion) is for the purpose of hearing a word or passage that touches the heart. When the word or phrase is found, it is silently taken in, and gently recited and pondered during the silence which follows. After the silence each person shares which word or phrase has touched his or her heart.

The second reading (by a member of the opposite sex from the first reader) is for the purpose of "hearing" or "seeing" Christ in the text. Each ponders the word that has touched the heart and asks where the word or phrase touches his or her life that day. In other words, how is Christ the Word touching their own experience, their own life? How are the various members of the group seeing or hearing

Christ reach out to them through the text? Then, after the silence, each member of the group shares what he or she has "heard" or "seen."

The third and final reading is for the purpose of experiencing Christ "calling us forth" into *doing* or *being*. Members ask themselves what Christ in the text is calling them to *do* or to *become* today or this week. After the silence, each shares for the last time; and the exercise concludes with each person praying for the person on the right.

Those who regularly practice this method of praying and sharing the Scriptures regularly find it to be an excellent way of developing trust within a group; it also is an excellent way of consecrating projects and hopes to Christ before more formal group meetings. A summary of this method for group *lectio divina* is appended at the end of this book (page 73).

Lectio Divina on Life

In the ancient tradition *lectio divina* was understood as being one of the most important ways in which Christians experience God in creation. After all, the Scriptures are part of creation! If one is daily growing in the art of finding Christ in the pages of the Bible, one naturally begins to discover the Lord more clearly in aspects of the other things. This includes, of course, our own personal history.

Our own lives are fit matter for *lectio divina*. Very often our concerns, our relationships, our hopes and aspirations naturally intertwine with our pondering on the Scriptures, as has been described above. But sometimes it is fitting to simply sit down and "read" the experiences of the last few days or weeks in our hearts, much as we might slowly read and savor the words of Scripture in *lectio divina*. We can attend "with the ear of our hearts" to our own memories, listening for God's gentle presence in the events of our lives. We thus allow ourselves the joy of experiencing Christ reach-

55

ing out to <u>us through our own memories</u>. Our own personal story becomes "salvation history."

For those who are new to the practice of *lectio divina*, a group experience of *"lectio* on life" can provide a helpful introduction. Such an approach is detailed at the end of this book. Like the experience of *lectio divina* shared in community, this group experience of *lectio* on life can foster relationships in community and enable personal experiences to be consecrated—offered to Christ—in a concrete way.

However, unlike scriptural *lectio divina* shared in community, this group *lectio* on life contains more silence than sharing. The role of group facilitators or leaders is important, since they will be guiding the group through several periods of silence and reflection without the "interruption" of individual sharing until the end of the exercise. Since the experiences we choose to "read" or "listen to" may be intensely personal, it is important in this group exercise to

safeguard privacy by making sharing completely optional.

In brief, one begins with restful silence,
then gently reviews the events of a given period of time. One seeks an event, a memory,
which touches the heart just as a word or
phrase in scriptural *lectio divina* does. One then
recalls the setting, the circumstances; one
seeks to discover how God seemed to be
present or absent from the experience. One
then offers the event to God and rests for a
time in silence. A suggested method for group
lectio divina on life is appended at the end of
this book (page 75).

Conclusion

*L*ectio divina is an ancient spiritual art that is being rediscovered in our day. It is a way of allowing the Scriptures to become again what God intended that they should be—a means of uniting us to God. In *lectio divina* we discover our own underlying spiritual rhythm. We experience God in a gentle oscillation back and forth between spiritual activity and receptivity, in the movement from practice into contemplation and back again into spiritual practice.

Lectio divina teaches us about the God who truly loves us. In *lectio divina* we dare to believe that our loving Father continues to extend an embrace to us today. And this embrace is real. In God's Word we experience ourselves as personally loved by God; as the recipients of a word which God gives uniquely to each of us whenever we turn to God in the Scriptures.

Finally, *lectio divina* teaches us about ourselves. In *lectio divina* we discover that there is no place in our hearts, no interior corner or closet that cannot be opened and offered to God. God teaches us in *lectio divina* what it means to be members of a royal priesthood— a people called to consecrate all of our memories, our hopes, and our dreams to Christ.

Appendices

APPENDIX 1

A Guide to Private Centering Prayer

S it comfortably in a chair that will give your back good support and gently close your eyes. It is well to choose a place where you will not be disturbed by any sudden intrusion. A quiet place is helpful, though not essential.

Three Rules or Guidelines

Sit relaxed and quiet.

1. Be in faith and love to God who dwells in the center of your being.
2. Take up a love word and let it be gently

present, supporting your being to God in faith-filled love.

3. Whenever you become aware of anything, simply, gently return to the Lord with the use of your prayer word.

Let the Our Father (or some other prayer) pray itself.

Centering Prayer lies within a living Christian tradition. Even the name has evolved through the centuries from the time of the early Christians who called it the *monologion*, or "one-word" prayer. It has been called Prayer of the Heart, Prayer of Simplicity, Prayer of Simple Regard, and so forth. And the presentation has been adapted to the people of each age. It is not surprising then that in our times it finds different presentations, largely because of the audience that is being served. Thus we now find Father Thomas Keating presenting Centering Prayer in a slightly different form, summing it up in four guidelines, followed by Ferdinand Mahfood's five-point presentation.

Father Thomas Keating's Four Guidelines

1. Choose a sacred word as the symbol of your intention to consent to God's presence and action within.
2. Sitting comfortably and with eyes closed, settle briefly and silently introduce the sacred word as the symbol of your consent to God's presence and action within us.
3. When you become aware of thoughts return ever-so-gently to the sacred word.
4. At the end of the prayer period, remain in silence with eyes closed for a couple of minutes.

Prayer of the Heart/ Centering Prayer

Ferdinand Mahfood's Five-Point Presentation

The Method. Make a commitment to the prayer—twenty minutes a day, twice each day for at least thirty days. It is best to set aside a prayer time which won't conflict with your schedule of daily routines. Find a quiet place where distractions are minimal.

1. Sit upright and relaxed in a comfortable chair. Close your eyes.
2. Be in faith and love to God. Many people begin with a simple opening prayer. For example:

   Lord, we thank you for your wonderful relationship with us. For these few minutes we want to be wholly with you. in love…in Christ.

3. Choose a single prayer word and let it be gently present, supporting your surrender to God in faith-filled love.
4. Whenever you become aware of any sound, emotion, or thought, simply return to the Lord through the gentle repetition of your prayer word.

5. After your prayer time has concluded, slowly, quietly say the Lord's Prayer. Let it bring a peaceful close to your time with God.

APPENDIX 2

A Guide to Group Centering Prayer

A group does best if it has a stable leader or leadership team. That does not mean that in the actual meeting the different members cannot take turns leading the prayer. Such alternation is good. Since new members are always invited to participate in the prayer group, a good policy is to begin each meeting with a brief introduction to Centering Prayer, giving the basic elements of the prayer. Following the introduction, I would suggest a format like this:

1. *Centering* for twenty minutes.

2. *Buzz session* of three to seven minutes, depending on the time available. This helps get the sharing and questions started.

3. *Break* of ten or fifteen minutes. Informal sharing.

4. *Question period*. It might be good to have a couple of common questions to lead off, in case the group is hesitant to raise questions; for example: How do you pick the word? Do you stay with it? How do you know if you are doing it wrong? How often is it good to pray this way? What if you skip?

5. A brief word on *lectio*.

6. *Centering*—perhaps preceded by some physical exercise.

7. Establish *follow-up*. In this step, resources that answer questions about the Centering experience are discussed, books and tapes on Centering Prayer are suggested for further study, continued participation in weekly group Centering Prayer is encouraged, and so on.

Appendix 3

A Guide to Private Lectio Divina

1. Take the sacred text with reverence, acknowledging God's presence, and call upon Holy Spirit.
2. For five minutes (or longer if you are so drawn) listen to the Lord speaking to you through the text and respond.
3. At the end of the time, choose a word or phrase (perhaps one will have been given to you) to take with you and thank the Lord for being with you and speaking to you.

APPENDIX 4

Two Approaches to Group Lectio Divina

Lectio Divina Shared in Community

Listening for the Gentle Touch of Christ the Word *(The Literal Sense)*

1. One person reads aloud (twice) the passage of Scripture, as others are attentive, choosing some segment that is especially meaningful to them.

2. *Silence* for 1–2 minutes. Each hears and silently repeats a word or phrase that attracts.

3. Sharing aloud: a word or phrase that has

attracted each person. A simple statement of one or a few words. *No elaboration.*

How Christ the Word Speaks to Me
(The Allegorical Sense)

4. Second reading of the same passage by a member of the opposite sex from the first reader.
5. *Silence* for 2–3 minutes. Reflect on "Where does this reading touch my life today?"
6. Sharing aloud: Briefly: "I hear, I see…."

What Christ the Word Invites Me to Do
(The Moral Sense)

7. Third reading by still another person.
8. *Silence* for 2–3 minutes. Reflect on "I believe that God wants me to _____ today/this week."
9. Sharing aloud: At somewhat greater length, the results of each person's reflection.
10. After full sharing, pray for one another.

Note: Anyone may "pass" at any time. If instead of sharing with the group you prefer to pray silently, simply state this aloud and conclude your silent prayer with *Amen*.

Lectio on Life

Applying Lectio Divina to My Personal Salvation History

The purpose of this group exercise is to apply a method of prayerful reflection to a life/work incident instead of to a Scripture passage.

Listen for the Gentle Touch of Christ the Word (*The Literal Sense*)

1. Each person quiets the body and mind: relax, sit comfortably but alert, close eyes, attune to breathing....
2. Each person gently reviews events, situations, sights, encounters that have happened since the beginning of the retreat or during the last month at work.

Gently Ruminating, Reflecting
(Meditatio—Meditation)

3. Each person allows the self to focus on one such offering.
   a) Recollect the setting, sensory details, sequence of events, and so on.
   b) Notice where the greatest energy seemed to be evoked. Was there a turning point or shift?
   c) In what ways did God seem to be present? To what extent was I aware then? Now?

Prayerful Consecration, Blessing
(Oratio—Prayer)

4. Use a word or phrase from the Scriptures to inwardly consecrate—to offer up to God in prayer—the incident and interior reflections. Allow God to accept and bless them as your gift.

Accepting Christ's Embrace;
Silent Presence to the Lord
(Contemplatio—Contemplation)

5. Remain in silence for some period.

Sharing Our *Lectio* Experience With Each Other *(Operatio—Action; Works)*

6. Leader calls the group back into "community."
7. All share briefly (though some individuals may freely choose to remain in continuing silence).

APPENDIX 5

Some Helpful Books and Audio Tapes

Books

BY THE SAME AUTHOR

Daily We Touch Him (Kansas City: Sheed & Ward, 1995).

Centering Prayer (New York: Doubleday, 1980).

A Place Apart (Liguori, MO: Liguori Publications, 1998).

Centered Living (Liguori, MO: Liguori Publications, 1999).

Lectio Divina (New York: Crossroad/Herder & Herder, 1998).

Living in the Question (New York: Continuum Pub Group, 1999).

Call to the Center (Hyde Park, NY: New City Press, 1990).

The Eucharist (Liguori, MO: Liguori Publications, 2000).

BY OTHER AUTHORS

The Cloud of Unknowing and the Book of Privy Counseling William Johnston, editor (New York: Doubleday, 1973).

Michael Casey, *Sacred Reading: The Ancient Art of Lectio Divina* (Liguori, MO: Triumph Books, 1996).

Thelma Hall, *Too Deep for Words: Rediscovering Lectio Divina* (Mahwah, NJ: Paulist Press, 1988).

Fr. Thomas Keating, O.C.S.O., *Open Mind, Open Heart* (Warwick NY: Amity House, 1986).

Fr. Henri Le Saux, O.S.B., *Prayer* (Philadelphia: Westminster Press, 1973).

Mariano Magrassi, Edward Hagman (Translator), *Praying the Bible: An Introduction to Lectio Divina* (Collegeville, MN: Liturgical Press, 1998).

Mario Masini, Edmund C. Lane (Translator), *Lectio Divina: An Ancient Prayer That Is Ever New* (New York: Alba House,1998).

Thomas Merton, *The Climate of Monastic Prayer* (Kalamazoo, MI: Cistercian Publications, 1968).

Francis Kelly Nemeck and Marie Theresa Coombs, *Contemplation* (Wilmington, DE: Glazier, 1982).

Ghislaine Salvail, Paul Duggan (Translator), *At the Crossroads of Scriptures: An Introduction to Lectio Divina* (Boston, MA: Daughters of St. Paul, 1996).

Tapes

BY THE SAME AUTHOR

"A Centered Life: A Practical Course on Centering Prayer," 16 conferences (Kansas City, MO: Credence Cassettes [National Catholic Reporter]).

"The Contemplative Attitude" (Kansas City, MO: Credence Cassettes [National Catholic Reporter]).

"Contemplation for Everyone," 3 conversations (Pompano, FL: Food for the Poor).

"A Matter of Love," 4 conversations (West Springfield, MA: Catholic Communications Office and Kansas City, MO: Credence Cassettes [National Catholic Reporter]).

"How To Center Your Life," 4 lectures (Allen, TX: Tabor [Argus] Communications).

By Other Authors

Thomas Keating, "Contemplative Prayer in the Christian Tradition: Historical Insights" (Spencer, MA: Joseph's Abbey); "The Spiritual Journey," 17 conferences (Colorado Springs, CO: Contemporary Communications).

William Meninger, "Contemplative Prayer," 4 conferences (Liguori, MO: Liguorian Press).

About the Authors

❦

Right Reverend Abbot Dom M. Basil Pennington, O.C.S.O. (AKA Robert John Pennington), was born in Brooklyn, New York, in 1931, the son of Dale Kelsey Pennington and Helene Josephine Kenny. He entered the Cistercian Order in 1951 at St. Joseph's Abbey, Spencer, Massachusetts, after graduating from Cathedral College of the Immaculate Conception and was consecrated a monk on September 8, 1956. After ordination in 1957 he spent several years in Rome gaining an S.T.L. and a J.C.L., winning two gold medals from Pope John XXIII. He assisted at the Second Vatican Council as a peritus and in the preparation of the new Code of Canon Law. With Thomas Merton he started Cistercian Publications in 1968 and founded the Institute of Cistercian

Studies at Western Michigan University in 1973. Father became known internationally through his efforts to help the Church refind its contemplative dimension through the Centering Prayer movement. For four years he served as the vocational father in his abbey, lecturing widely and publishing a book on vocational discernment. In 1983, in collaboration with leaders from other churches and the synagogue, he formed the Mastery Foundation for the empowering of those whose lives are about sacred ministry. From 1986 to 1989 he served at Assumption Abbey in Ava, Missouri. In 1991 he went to help his Chinese brethren at Our Lady of Joy Monastery, Lantao, where he served until 1998, while continuing his worldwide ministry in Centering Prayer. Father has published over fifty books and almost a thousand articles in various languages. His most recent publications are *The Abbey Prayer Book* (Liguori, 2002), *The Eucharist* (Liguori, 2000), *Lectio Divina: Renewing the Ancient Practice of Praying the Scriptures* (Crossroad) and *Living in the Question* (Continuum). Father Basil was appointed superior of Assumption Abbey in January 2000 and elected abbot of Our Lady of Holy Spirit Abbey (Conyers, Georgia) the following August.

Luke Dysinger, O.S.B., is a Benedictine monk of Saint Andrew's Abbey, Valyermo, in Southern California. Before joining the monastery in 1980, Father practiced medicine as a family practitioner and taught biomedical ethics. In the past he has served his monastic community as prior, master of novices, and director of vocations. He is presently juniormaster and librarian. In 2000, he received his D.Phil. in theology from Oxford University, specializing in the writings of Evagrius Ponticus. In addition to writing in the field of patristics he gives retreats and workshops; and he teaches moral theology and church history at St. John's Seminary, the diocesan seminary for the Archdiocese of Los Angeles.

Finished A.M.
Monday May 2, 2005
NSB

Mon. 04/25/05

retreat@trappist.net

$30 non-refunda donatio to hold rooms. Suggeste offering of $60-7 per night

Our Lady of The Holy Spirit Monastery * **

2625 Highway 212 S.W.

Conyers, GA 30094-4044

phone: 770-483-8705

Fax: 770-760-0989

E-Mail: monastery@trappist.net

"IF This is beyond your means, please come anyway and give as much as you are able credit cards o

*(35 miles East of Atlanta)

"The Monastery of The Holy Spirit is a Roman Catholic monastery of The Cistercian Order of The Strict Observance (represented by The abbreviation OCSO).

Our order's constitutions give a concise description of our monastic life as Cistercians:

This order is a monastic institute wholly ordered to contemplation. The monks dedicate Themselves to The Worship of God in a hidden life within The monastery under The Rule of St. Benedict. They lead a monastic way of life in Solitude and silence, in assiduous prayer and joyful penitence."

** contacted Them by email re: retreats in Sept. 2005 Mon. 04/25/05 @ 1:00 PM.

"The monastery of the Holy Spirit invites you to come and experience a few days of restful recollection and spiritual renewal in a prayerful and peaceful environment. ... to listen in silence to The Holy Spirit bringing guidance and enlightenment. These and other experiences can be yours according to god's gift. Above all, your time of retreat is to help you experience The love of God for you. (emphasis mine). The benefits, may be summed up in of a retreat The word peace - God's peace which surpasses all understanding.